Sharks

Catriona Clarke
Designed by Stephen Moncrieff
Illustrated by Adam Relf

Additional illustrations by Ian West
Reading consultant: Alison Kelly, Roehampton University

Contents

All kinds of sharks

There are more than 400 different types of sharks. Some are as big as a bus and some are as small as this book.

This tiger shark is twice as big as a grown man.

What is a shark?

A shark is a type of fish. Lots of sharks look like this blacktip reef shark.

Snout

Gills

These two fins help the shark to turn, and swim up or down.

A shark's skeleton isn't made of bone, like other fish. It is made of cartilage, which is lighter and bendier.

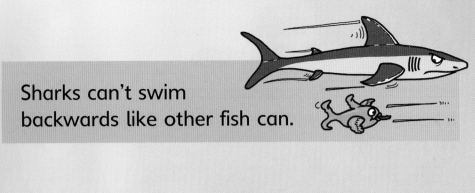

Sharks can't swim backwards like other fish can.

The fin on the shark's back stops it rolling from side to side.

The tail fin helps the shark to swim quickly.

Gill power

All animals need a gas called oxygen to live. Sharks and other fish use their gills to take oxygen from the water around them.

Some sharks keep their mouths open while they're swimming, to let water flow in.

The shark takes in oxygen as the water flows out through the gill slits.

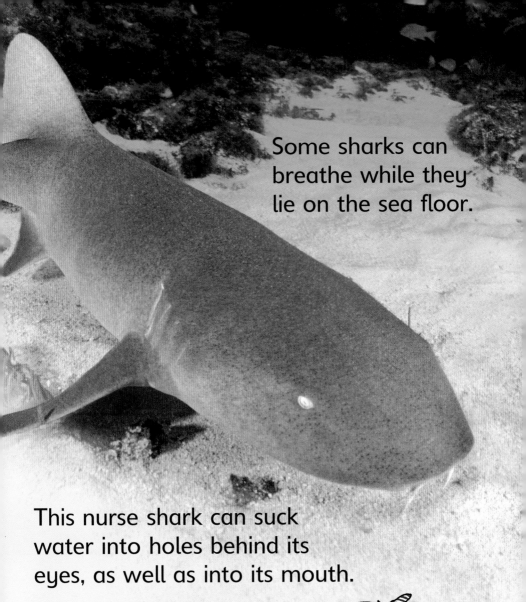

Some sharks can
breathe while they
lie on the sea floor.

This nurse shark can suck
water into holes behind its
eyes, as well as into its mouth.

Some sharks need to keep
swimming to be able to breathe.
They even swim in their sleep!

Super senses

Sharks are the best hunters in the ocean. They have very good hearing, eyesight and sense of smell.

A struggling fish caught on a fishing line makes sound waves in the water that a shark can hear from a long way away.

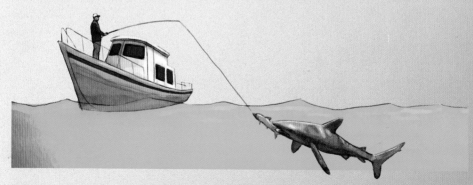

The shark quickly moves in to attack. It snatches the fish from the fisherman's line and eats it.

Sharks also have extra senses that help them to find food.

All animals give off small electric signals. There are tiny holes on this shark's snout. These allow it to sense signals coming from a fish hiding nearby.

Types of teeth

A shark's main weapon is its teeth. Sharks have different shapes of teeth depending on what they eat.

Great white sharks have huge, jagged teeth for cutting into big chunks of meat.

Sand tiger sharks have sharp, pointed teeth for holding small, struggling fish.

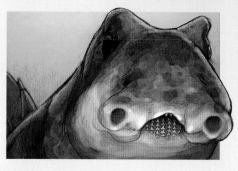

A hornshark has small, flat teeth for cracking and grinding shells.

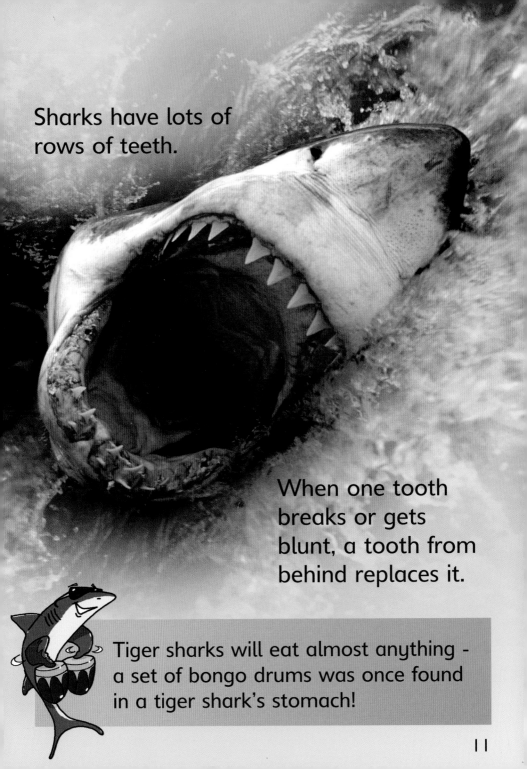

Sharks have lots of rows of teeth.

When one tooth breaks or gets blunt, a tooth from behind replaces it.

Tiger sharks will eat almost anything - a set of bongo drums was once found in a tiger shark's stomach!

Attack!

Some sharks surprise their prey by rushing at it from below.

Each year, baby albatrosses learn to fly on beaches near Hawaii, USA.

Tiger sharks lurk beneath the surface, waiting for a bird to fall or land in the water.

A shark bursts out of the water and attacks an unlucky baby albatross.

Sharks sometimes attack people, but this is very rare.

This surfboard was bitten by a tiger shark, but the surfer escaped.

A thresher shark can use its long tail fin to hit its prey before eating it.

Different disguises

Many sharks can hide from their prey because of the way they look.

They have dark backs, which make them difficult to spot from the surface.

They have pale bellies, which make them hard to see from below, too.

14

Scientists have discovered that scalloped hammerhead sharks can get a suntan!

Tasselled wobbegong sharks are very well disguised.

Their patterned skin helps them to blend in with the rocks on the sea floor.

Baby sharks

Baby sharks are called pups. Some pups hatch from eggs and some are born like other animals.

This is the egg case of a dogfish shark.

This pup will hatch out in a few months.

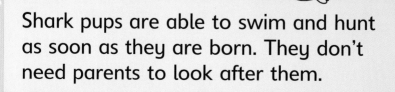

Shark pups are able to swim and hunt as soon as they are born. They don't need parents to look after them.

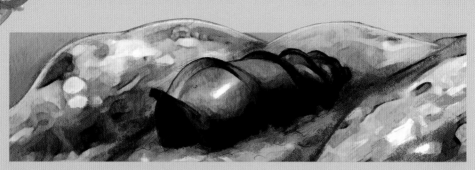

A hornshark lays strange-looking eggs that are shaped like spirals.

It pushes the eggs into gaps between the rocks to keep them safe from danger.

Eight months later, the pups break out of the egg cases and swim away.

Across the oceans

Sharks live in all the oceans of the world. Some sharks like to stay in one place. This place is called their territory.

Caribbean reef sharks live near coral reefs where the water is warm.

Greenland sharks live in the icy cold water near the North Pole.

Bull sharks sometimes swim a very long way up rivers.

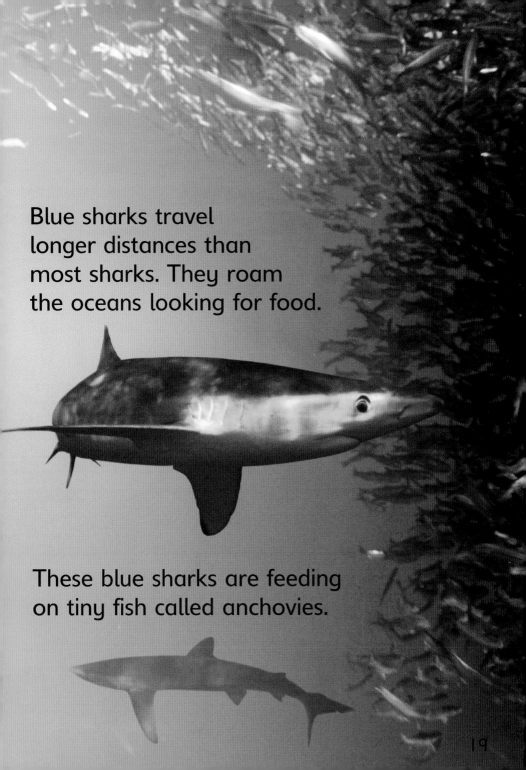

Blue sharks travel
longer distances than
most sharks. They roam
the oceans looking for food.

These blue sharks are feeding
on tiny fish called anchovies.

Sharks of the deep

There are sharks that live far below the surface of the ocean.

This is a frilled shark. Its
long body makes it
look like an eel.

Scientists do not know
much about frilled sharks,
because they hardly ever see them.

The shark above is a prickly dogfish. It has sharp spines in front of its fins.

A lanternshark's body glows in the darkness of the deep ocean.

Gentle giants

The biggest sharks of all are also the least dangerous. They feed on small fish and tiny animals and plants called plankton.

The whale shark is the biggest fish in the world.

It swims just beneath the surface of the water.

It feeds by swimming with its huge mouth open. It takes food from the water as the water flows out through its gills.

Whale sharks can grow to be the size of a bus.

Great white terror

The great white shark is the most famous shark. It eats big fish, seals, sea lions, dolphins and sometimes even people.

This cage allows a diver to stay safe while studying the shark.

A great white shark can go without food for two months after it has eaten a big meal.

A great white shark circles a group of seals before it moves in for the kill.

The shark attacks. It thrusts its jaws forward, so that it can take a huge bite.

It leaps out of the water and snaps its jaws shut around the seal.

Strange sharks

Some sharks look very different from the normal shark shape.

A swellshark swells up its body and wedges itself between rocks so that it can't be attacked.

Sawsharks have long snouts.

They use their snouts to find prey buried in the sand.

Hammerhead sharks like to eat all kinds of fish, especially rays.

The shark uses its wide head to pin down a ray. Then, it bites the ray's wing.

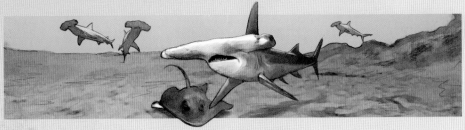

Now that the ray can't swim away, the shark can take its time to eat it.

Sharks in danger

Millions of sharks are killed each year. Some types of shark are in danger of completely dying out if this doesn't change.

Some people like to try to catch big, dangerous sharks for sport.

In many countries sharks are killed for their fins, which are used to make soup.

Oil leaking from ships and other kinds of pollution can poison sharks.

Sharks also get tangled up in fishing nets. They die because they cannot breathe.

This silky shark has been trapped in a net used for catching tuna.

Glossary of shark words

Here are some of the words in this book you might not know. This page tells you what they mean.

 gills - slits on a shark's body that help it to breathe underwater.

 snout - a shark's nose. Sharks use their snouts to help them find food.

 prey - the fish or other creatures that a shark hunts and eats.

 pup - a baby shark. Some sharks have over a hundred pups.

 egg case - a hard shell that shark pups live in before they hatch.

 territory - the place where a shark lives most of the time.

 plankton - tiny animals and plants. Whale sharks eat plankton.

Websites to visit

You can visit exciting websites to find out more about sharks.

To visit these websites, go to the Usborne Quicklinks website at **www.usborne.com/quicklinks**
Read the internet safety guidelines, and then type the keywords "**beginners sharks**".

The websites are regularly reviewed and the links in Usborne Quicklinks are updated. However, Usborne Publishing is not responsible, and does not accept liability, for the content or availability of any website other than its own. We recommend that children are supervised while on the internet.

This shark tooth is millions of years old. In real life, it is bigger than your hand.

Index

Acknowledgements

Photographic manipulation by John Russell

Photo credits

The publishers are grateful to the following for permission to reproduce material: cover © **Stephen Frink Collection/Alamy**; p1 © **Chris & Monica Fallows/Seapics.com**; p2-3 © **Stuart Westmorland/Corbis**; p4-5 © **Franco Banfi/Seapics.com**; p7 © **Masa Ushioda/ Seapics.com**; p9 © **Chris & Monica Fallows/Seapics.com**; p11 © **Stephen Frink/Alamy**; p13 © **Adrien Warren/Ardea**; p15 © **Gary Bell/Seapics.com**; p16 © **Douglas P Wilson/Frank Lane Picture Agency/CORBIS**; p19 © **Richard Herrmann/Seapics.com**; p20-21 © **Photoshot**; p21 © **Rudie Kuiter/Seapics.com**; p22-23 © **Louie Psihoyos/Corbis**; p24-25 © **Jeff Rotman/ naturepl.com**; p26-27 © **Stephen Frink Collection/Alamy**; p29 © **Stephen Frink Collection/ Alamy**; p31 © **DK Limited/Corbis**